Access is the Key to Success

DAVID K. CRAWFORD

ISBN 1-931600-77-5

Endorsements

This book could be the turning point in your life. The wisdom in these pages is so very important to your personal success. Pastor David Crawford lives what he teaches. It has been my privilege to be his personal friend for a number of years. His revelation is like fresh air in a stagnant world. It is a privilege to recommend this book to every person who treasures favor and success. Read it carefully and often. Your pursuit of this wisdom will not go unrewarded.

Dr. Dave Martin
Dave Martin International / Orlando, Florida

Pastor Crawford has presented a powerful theme of limiting access in your life to empower goals and change. Motivating and easy to read with great stories, you will enjoy his message!

Charlotte U. Fleming, Esq.

I thought that I would sit down and read a page or two a day, but I sat down and couldn't put it down. Pastor David Crawford has written a filter by which we as a people can determine what to permit access into our lives and what we should refrain from entrance. I believe this should be a part of monthly devotional and study reading. I was inspired to guard my heart with all diligence.

Tim Gidley
Tim Gidley Ministries, Inc.

Over the years I have watched many young men receive the call of God and begin their ministry journey. As problems and obstacles arise unfortunately many become discouraged, disillusioned and even quit. I have personally watched Pastor David Crawford, as he has encountered ministry and personal battles. Some were of the nature that he could easily have given way to bitterness and resentment, but he has always walked through each challenge with personal growth and a greater anointing upon his life. This young man has learned some principles of leadership and it is a joy to recommend his insight to you.

Robert E. Turner
District Superintendent / Tennessee Assemblies of God

Dedication

One of the greatest examples of mentoring is the Apostle Paul. He truly understood the importance of mentoring and invested in many young men called into the ministry. There is another Paul that understood the art of mentoring. This Paul never saw Jesus on the road to Damascus, although he saw the call of Christ in the lives of young men and women. This Paul was not educated by Gamaliel, but he spent many years in the classroom of the Holy Spirit. This Paul was never led before Agrippa, although he was tried and tested throughout forty-five years of ministry. Just as Paul had his Timothy, this Paul had many young "Timothys."

Rev. Paul E. McKeel had a heart for young preachers. Of all the great men of my life, and there have been many, this Paul had care and concern for the call of God on a young man's life, and a love for people to help cultivate that call. His ministry never incorporated, nor did he hire a marketing firm to expand "his ministry." Although at the time it did not seem world-wide, his ministry lives on in the lives of all the men and women in which he invested his time, wisdom, and experience. It was never strange for this Paul to spend hours in a wood shop, to take trips in his pick-up, or spend time in the office sharing the love of God and the joy of the ministry to some young minister. It was not uncommon for this Paul to reach in the gutters of discouragement and pull out a person in whom he sensed a call of God and love them back to ministry. Rev. Paul E. McKeel shared his mistakes and mountaintops, his failures and achievements, his heartbeat and his dreams. He was busy. He had people to visit, meetings to make, a church to run, but he always had time for someone who needed counsel. His investment truly lives on!

**This book is dedicated in memory of Rev. Paul E McKeel
1933 – 1996.**

Table of Contents

Acknowledgements

We cannot fulfill Christ's mission alone as individuals. People are vital to God! He has always been interested in building people. Nothing is more important than that. God is a people builder! That is why I am thankful for the people God has brought into my life. Their access has caused me to think and challenged me on toward the completion of this book and my principal priorities.

The first person that I want to thank is Kristen Ross Smith. Your ability to cut through the issues, pinpoint objectives, and stay focused has helped me be more concise and effective. Your attention to detail and specifics of instruction contributed greatly to the clarity and effectiveness of this book. It would not have happened without your help. You are inspiring!

Freeman and Charlotte Crawford (Mom and Dad) whom, despite your own physical limitations, outclassed and surpassed others with no limitations. Thanks for the constant inspiration, encouragement, and the occasional kick in the pants.

I want to express my love for the most significant person in my life, my sunshine and best friend, DeAnna. You give my life meaning while making it fun. Your ability to critique and challenge me has been an encouragement that has pressed me toward my dreams. Your love has been a motivating strength that is and always has been compelling me forward, regardless of the circumstances.

To my booger-bear, Danielle: You have wisdom, perception, and an incredible prophetic gifting. Daddy is so proud of you and the call of God on your life.

S. Ott Denney, the most incredible assistant in the world, possibly the galaxy. Without your help this book would not exist, nor look as good as it does.

Because English is not my first language and my typing skills are archaic, Thank you Michelle Cobb, James Ellis, Tamara Jones, Kristen Kelly, and DeAnna Crawford for your help in the editing process.

Thank you, Daniel Scobey, for your marketing and advertising insights and most of all for being a dear friend.

Pastors, Ministry Directors, and Council of Elders of River Community Church, thank you for sharing your bishop with others. Your dedication is an inspiration.

To the countless mentors, known and unknown, may this book, which may ring with familiar wisdom be a complement to your ministries. Thanks for your investment.

I would like to personally thank some of my very special partners who helped sponsor this project through their generous gifts:

Arlin & Kris Smith

Buddy & Cathey Hill

James & Colleen Ellis

Joe & Christy Hunter

Ott & Kristen Denney

Eddie & Pam Crawford

Foreword

Dr. Paul Crites

I stepped off the plane in Nashville, Tennessee, to speak that weekend at River Community Church. As I cleared security I met David Crawford. His gracious manner and winning smile made for a warm welcome. He quickly grabbed my briefcase, and escorted me down stairs to secure my bags. Most places just send someone to drive you to the hotel, but this was not most places, and I would soon learn David Crawford was not like most people. The scene I just described repeated itself several more times that same year.

David Crawford understands access, protocol, and success with people. He has stood the test of time during great adversity and challenge. We have prayed together, laughed together, and walked through valleys and mountain tops together. Despite the difficulty, David Crawford always remains the same man; positive and focused. He has discovered a key that has been enlarged upon in the pages you are about to read.

The key is access.

It would be my prayer that leaders, educators, pastors, and entrepreneurs everywhere would digest the contents of this book. It is so easy to lose focus and access to the very ones we are trying to serve...that is why what David Crawford has to say is so important.

I stood on the platform of River Community Church a few months ago as David's congregation honored him upon receiving one of his postgraduate degrees. I watched as everyone extended congratulations and hearty hugs. It was a wonderful time. I also observed our friend David Crawford, walk over to several young boys and girls and take the time to encourage them about their educational pursuits. He had each one have a photograph taken with him as he gave them access into his world of celebration that evening.

I am honored to call him my friend and very happy that he made a decision long ago to give me access into his life and ministry. After you read this book I am certain you will feel the same.

Introduction

The American writer and physician Oliver Wendell Holmes advised us, "To reach the port of success we must sail, sometimes with the wind and sometimes against it — but we must sail, not drift or lie at anchor." Your success is my destiny. To most, the first thought that enters their minds when you speak of success, is financial independence. In fact, most suppose to be successful is to be grossly wealthy. Although being financially collected is part of being successful it is not the sum total.

American president Theodore Roosevelt gave a speech early in the 20th century where he acknowledged some practical insights about success: "There are two kinds of success. One is the very rare kind that comes to the man who has the power to do what no one else has the power to do. That is genius. But the average man who wins what we call success is not a genius. He is a man who has merely the ordinary qualities that he shares with his fellows, but who has developed those ordinary qualities to a more than ordinary degree." Success is not just something that happens. Success is something that you plan for. Success is defined as the, "achievement of something planned or attempted."

I agree with John Maxwell's definition of success, "Success is knowing your purpose in life, growing to reach your maximum potential, and sowing seeds that benefit others." The book of Proverbs says, "Maintain a balanced life and you will be successful." Your preparation for success is not necessarily about a wall of degrees earned from years of formal education. Much more important is whether you were a serious student or just taking up space in a succession of meaningless classes. Whether your education is formal or informal does not matter as much as your determination to become self-educated and balanced. You are responsible for you!

As you read this book get ready for peace and prosperity. Get ready to live a life of conviction and purpose. The Scottish essayist Thomas Carlyle wrote, "Have a purpose in life, and throw yourself into your work with all the strength of mind and muscle God has given." Get ready to be successful.

John Wooden, the famous basketball coach, advises us, "Don't measure yourself by what you have accomplished but by what you should have accomplished with your ability." I once saw a man shooting with a compound bow at a foam deer with his two little boys excitingly cheering him on. As they were watching their dad shoot, they would jump and clap as he hit the deer. Why were they rejoicing? They were rejoicing because he had a target and he hit it. You cannot walk through life just shooting wherever you want and then draw a circle around it and say that was your target. But that is how a lot of people are living. If you happened upon any type of success, you have done it by accident. When you fail to plan, you plan to fail. Success is the achievement of something that you have planned for or have attempted.

Access is the key to success. What does access have to do with success? Access is the control of time, and time is your life. Therefore, becoming a master of your time and who you allow access to it is essential for your success. The greatest treasure you have is your control of access. Access is not time management, it is self-management. Access is further defined as, "an entry or an approach. It is the opportunity, the experience, or use of something." You could say it this way; it is a right to meet someone or exchange with someone.

The French Emperor Napoleon observed, "There is one kind of robber whom the law does not strike at, and who steals what is most precious: Time." Time is not a renewable resource. God has given us all the same measure of time and the free will to use it. You do not want to squander this precious gift. This is your one opportunity at life. You repay God by becoming an effective time manager and leading an exemplary life.

Chapter 1

Your Success Is Determined By Knowing Your Purpose And Limiting Access

Access, like purpose and passion, must be protected. II Timothy, 1:14 says, "Guard the good deposit that was entrusted to you. Guard it with the help of the Holy Spirit who lives in us." Access is the key to success. You just read that we have to guard what has been entrusted to our care. Paul went on to say, "Timothy, guard what has been entrusted to your care. Turn away from godless chatter and the opposing ideas of what is falsely called knowledge which some have professed and some are doing and they are wandering in faith." Wandering is BAD! Cain killed Abel and he wandered. The children of Israel disobeyed God and they wandered. If you are wandering around in life, it is a good sign that you have a curse on your life. You need to stop wandering and let your steps be ordered by the Lord. You need to let God direct you. You need to find out what your destiny is, what your purpose is, and begin to fulfill it.

What is the "good deposit" of God? The deposit of God is your gifting. It is your revelation. It is your anointing. It is your appointing. It is your teaching. It is your preaching. It is what God, by the power of the Holy

Spirit, has deposited in you to make you who you are, and to equip you to do the work of the ministry. That means there is a lot of work for you to do. There is a purpose that God has established for you. Paul says, "Guard what the Holy Spirit has given you. What he has put inside you." What I am saying is this: your experiences – times of joy and pain – qualify you to help others. The anointing of God is upon your life. That may be a revelation to some of you, but it is. Paul is saying you must protect what the Holy Spirit has deposited into you. How do you guard it? He goes on to say, with the "Help of the Holy Spirit who lives in us"; the Holy Spirit will help you, and enable you to guard what you have been given.

Paul instructed Timothy, his young protégé in the faith, to "entrust my teaching (or my deposits) to reliable men." He did not say every man. He did not say everybody. He said reliable men. I am sure it will come as no surprise to you that not everyone is reliable.

People walk around focusing on the part of John 8:32, which deals with truth setting people free. Does truth really set people free? If truth sets people free, then why are drug addicts still addicted? If truth sets people free, why are alcoholics still addicted? Addicts know the truth and understand where their life is going. They know that drugs will kill them. If you have ever sat down with one of them, they will tell you, "I want to be free", but that truth does not set them free. There is a key to that passage of scripture in John 8:31,32. "To the

Jews that had believed him," Jesus said, then he lays out the requirement of the scripture we go around quoting, "if you hold to my teaching you are really my disciples. Then you will know the truth and the truth will set you free." We quote that scripture yet we forget all the qualifiers before that scripture. The point is not just knowing the truth, but applying it. Access focuses on your application of the revelation not just the expansion of your information.

The following are examples of two ways which people respond to the truth. One is an illustration of an expansion of information, and the other is an illustration of the application of the revelation.

Expanding Information: A woman came to our church services one Sunday and felt the power of God. The following week she insisted her daughter, Susan, come with her. Susan sat while the presence and the power of God moved in our service. I remember her coming to the altar as she began to weep. After I led Susan to the Lord, she said to me, "Pastor, I can't believe you would pray with me. I had to shoot up a little before I came in to church tonight so I wouldn't get the shakes while I was here. I know you probably want me to leave now." My reply was absolutely not. At the end of that service, I sat her down on the first pew and I said, "Susan, tonight you have started a process, but it is a lifelong process. You need to allow what Jesus has done in your life to begin to take root. I want to take you to Teen Challenge, and get you placed into a program so that you can be set free from drugs." Susan did not want to go and leave her friends, her town, or the heroin. Just a few years ago I got a report that a drug deal went bad and they found Susan with her back broken, totally beaten up, lying on her kitchen floor dead. You can say, "Pastor, she came to an altar. She heard the truth." Yes, but she did not believe. You have to believe the truth, and then you have to follow the teachings of Christ. "Then the truth will set you free." (John 8:32) Susan expanded her information, but like a lot of people, never applied the revelation that would have brought change and success to her life.

Applying the Revelation: Before preaching at a revival service I was praying, "Lord, send somebody my way. Devil, I serve notice to you that I am going to go down the street, and speak to every person I see until I win someone to Christ." At that moment, I heard the pastor talking to someone. I said, "This is my man! God sent him. He is here. This is awesome! This is great! It is a miracle!"

The man's name was Sam. He was telling the pastor, "I just got out of jail. I got busted for having crack and I am strung out. I don't know what to do. My momma, she don't love me no more and that's why I am doing..." I interrupted, "Sam, My name is David Crawford. It is not your momma's fault, it is not your daddy's fault, it is not the sheriff's fault, it is not the sheriff's department's fault. It is your fault, partner. And if you can realize that it is your fault, I can help you change your

4

life. Do you know what you need? You do not need to be concerned about 25 years in jail. You need to be concerned about hell." Tears began to stream down his face. He said, "Well what do I need to do?" I told him he needed to ask Jesus into his heart. So we knelt down right there in the middle of the church foyer and he said the sinner's prayer.

Sam got up and I said, "We are having revival tonight and you need to be here. I wrote down where he lived and how to get there and I said, "If you are not here at 7:00, I'm coming to get you." That night as praise and worship was beginning I looked for Sam- 7:05, 7:10, 7:15 rolled around. As I began to walk off the platform to find Sam, I saw him walk in the back door with a lady and a little baby. The family sat on the back pew. I looked at the pastor with a big smile on my face and said, "Wow. Sam made it. That tells me what is really going on in his heart."

Suddenly Sam walked down to the front and looked up at me. I went down there and I said, "Sam, we are trying to have a service here." He said, "I know it. I spent my last $30 renting the hotel room that I was arrested in because when they came in, I stashed the drugs. I knew that if I did not go back and get those drugs then that hotel room would be like a magnet to me for the rest of my life. I would always have something to go back to. So I checked back in to that hotel room so I could get the drugs. I brought them and I want you to have them." He put four big rocks of crack in my hand. I have never touched drugs in my entire life and I thought, "What in the world am I going to do with this?"

Suddenly I had an idea. In scripture, when they brought all the old scrolls to the apostles they set them on fire. So I said, "Yes Lord! I know what we're going to do." It's truly amazing what you will do under the anointing.

Here was this guy that said, "I want to be free. I am not going to have anything hanging over my head for the rest of my life. I spent my last $30 so I could go get these drugs and put them in the hands of a preacher." I'm talking about somebody that really wanted to be set free! Man I got excited. I grabbed some tissues, wrapped the drugs up, and put them in the middle of a platter. I took anointing oil and poured it on the drugs. Then I set them on fire. Sam, who had never been in a Pentecostal church in his life, had his hands in the air and he began to shout, "I'm free! I'm free! I'm free!" Tears were streaming down his face. I ran over to Sam and said, "When God takes something out he'll put something back in. You are about to get filled with the Holy Ghost." I laid hands on him and he fell out under the power of God and began to speak in tongues.

All of a sudden I began to smell something that was not quite right. Then it dawned on me; that is how you do those drugs. You smoke them. So I grabbed that stuff, flames going all over the place, and flung it out an emergency exit door. The church stood to their feet and began shouting. I thought in my mind, "Oh Lord! I got

6

one free and the rest hooked." I prayed, "Oh, Jesus! Set them free!" I thought, "There go my credentials, there goes my ministry. Oh God set them free!"

Then the lady and the child came up to the front and she said, "I'm Sam's ex-wife and I want to give my life to Jesus Christ like Sam did today." I led her to the Lord. When the service ended their marriage was restored. Do you know what Sam does today? He now manages his own company.

Access will not allow you to draw yesterday into your future. What is the difference between Susan and Sam? He believed in Jesus Christ, chose to follow the teachings of Jesus Christ, and the truth set him free. Susan did not really want to be free because when presented with the opportunity and confronted with the truth she chose not to apply the revelation. She did not want to be guided by the simple rules that would have brought freedom to her life like Sam did. There is a big difference. Access will cause you to be ruled by the rules.

Chapter 2

Limited Access Will Keep You Focused On Your Assignment

The greatest treasure you can give someone is access into your life. Access is giving the right to encounter or exchange with someone, and you hold the keys to that access. Therefore access must be qualified. The Christian is always saying, "Well, we are called to everybody... the whosoever wills..." Have you ever thought about that statement? Whosoever will? That means there are some "whosoever will nots." Just because you are a Christian you do not have to let negative people and negative influences into your life. People are like elevators they will either take you up, or take you down. Yes, you have to love everybody! But you do not have to let everybody on your elevator! We are not called to everybody, but we are called to somebody and that is a big difference.

Was Jesus called to everyone? Look at Matthew 9:9-11. "And Jesus went on from there, he saw a man named Matthew sitting at the tax collectors booth. 'Follow me,' he told them, and Matthew got up and followed Him. While Jesus was having dinner at Matthew's house, many tax collectors and 'sinners' came and ate with him and his disciples. When the Pharisees saw this, they asked his disciples, 'Why does your teacher eat with tax collectors and 'sinners'?'" In other words, why is He hanging out with those people? Does He not know who they are? He knew who they were because they were His assignment, and the Pharisees were not.

Jesus was a religious leader but He was not called to the religious people. In fact, it was the religious people that perturbed Him the most. That is why He was not giving the Pharisees access to his time. The only time in scripture that He gave them access was when they confronted Him in public, because He was not called to everybody, He was called to somebody.

Look back at Matthew. "On hearing this, Jesus said, 'It is not the healthy that need a doctor, but the sick'."(Matthew 9:12) Jesus had a purpose. He knew his assignment and He was not going to let anything else break His focus. People will also come into your life trying to distract, delay, and discourage your focus when you allow improper access. Do not let anyone trivialize your passion. Allow no one access that does not promote success.

Who do you let have access into your life? Where does your time go? These are some of the things that we are going to begin to discuss. You must realize that you do not have to let everybody have access into your life, because if you do your life is going to be a mess. Some associations have come to break your focus, and distract you from doing what you are supposed to be doing.

Sometimes there are people that come into your life and do nothing but tear you down. Allowing the wrong or unwanted person access into your life will hinder your productivity. Limited access will keep you focused on your assignment.

You do not let just anybody in your home, so why do you let just anybody into your life? You would not let someone that is sick hold one of your babies, yet you let people that are just as sick and/or diseased in their spirit have all kinds of access into your heart and life. Access, like purpose and passion, must be protected. The main person responsible for your success is you.

Chapter 3

Your Success Is Determined By Whom/What Has Access To Your Time

One year contains 525,600 minutes, 1,440 minutes in each day. Having a lack of time is not the problem, but having a sense of direction and using your time wisely are the critical factors. Your success is determined by those whom you let have access to those minutes. Those who enjoy success control the access of their time. Remember, the greatest treasure you can give someone is access. People that do not respect your time will not respect your wisdom either. Too often we let other things and other people consume our time. Giving someone access that is not your assignment is dangerous. Paul told Timothy to take the things that he had seen, take the teachings, take his deposit, and pass it on to reliable men that would teach others. In other words, only give what I have given you to people that are going to be producers, people that are going to bear fruit, people that are going to take what you have taught them, and apply it to their life and teach others. Mastering time is choosing to live your life consciously and being aware of what you are doing and why you are doing it.

Access is the only influence that you have in your life. Proverbs 12:26 says, "A righteous man is cautious with his friendships." Your assignment needs your access. Those to whom you are called, the people that are producing, should be the people to whom you are ministering. Access will motivate passion and enthusiasm for your assignment. But, if you give access to the wrong person then the right person cannot get to you.

Be a person of controlled access. Demand excellence of yourself in all your endeavors. Focus your energy on things that you have the authority over, or the ability to directly change, like your ability to show up at work on time, because you want to be a good example of Godly character and integrity. The enemy will try to come and break focus in your life. Then somewhere in the process, you find yourself giving your time, energy, and focus to something that you cannot change.

Great ideas never die; they just lose the energy to complete them. Too many priorities will paralyze you. When the lion-tamers get in the cage with the lions they have a chair. When they hold the chair out the lion will just sit there. If they pull the whip out the lion will slap at that whip. Why? It is only one target. When the lion-tamers hold a four-legged chair out the lion does not know which leg to swing at so do you know what he does? Nothing. Our response is similar to that of the lion when we have too many priorities, when there is too much to do; we just end up doing nothing. Too many priorities paralyze us.

Access is extremely important when it comes to self-management. I want to give you five rules of self-management that will draw you toward your destiny.

Access Requires Intense Planning. Initially, goal setting and planning may seem like a lot of work. However, this is not a step to skip or to take for granted. Access plans for the unexpected. It takes 21 days to establish a habit whether good or bad. Start today to write daily goals and in 21 days you will have begun to form an important positive habit. In these few short weeks, goal setting and planning will begin to become second nature. You consider options. You make choices. You gain confidence. With confidence, you become even better at decision-making. You become increasingly proficient in separating the urgent and the important from the interesting but inconsequential.

Access Will Cause Organization of Schedules and Appointments. The American statesman Benjamin Franklin said, "Lost time is never found again." God did not give you relationships. He gave you time to invest in people so that you can create relationships. Access to your time becomes the great exchange. Your appointments constitute your interaction with other people. They are the agreed upon interface between your activities and those of others. Someone has well said that it is impossible to save time - you must simply learn to invest it wisely.

Be ruthless and eliminate the unnecessary. There may be committees where you cannot productively contribute or where a subordinate might be better able to participate. There may be long lunches that could be run as short conference calls. Eliminate the waste starting today. The single most important type of activity is those which will save you time. It is essential to allocate time to save time. A simple stitch in time saves days. It is very important to always allocate time-to-time management: I suggest at least ten minutes each and every day.

Access Will Eliminate Any Appointment or Request That Does Not Qualify for Your Focus. The American Writer Henry David Thoreau wrote, "It is not enough to be busy; so are the ants. The question is: What are we busy about?" You must guard access by qualifying those you allow to enter your life. When you eliminate appointments that break focus and lead to disorganization then you cause your day to be productive. Gordon MacDonald in his book, *Ordering Your Private World,* says, "Disorganized Christians rarely enjoy intimacy with God." It is not about their intentions or even their knowing that they should set aside time to be with God. They know that they should spend their time wisely focused on their God given purpose, but they are simply not doing it. Eliminating needless appointments from your schedule frees your time for essential activities.

Access Will Cause You to Delegate Tasks to Others. You can accomplish more when you involve others. Whether you are leading your family, or a major corporation, you must be able to delegate assignments.

Delegating means to pass responsibility of a task to others. Delegating helps you to concentrate on what you do best and allows you to think, plan and improve organizational efficiency. You delegate tasks that are cost and time effective for others to do for you. You also delegate tasks that people can do better than you can do. The American President Harry Truman said, "It is amazing what you can accomplish if you do not care who gets the credit."

Access Will Cause You to Focus on the Difference Between the Important and the Urgent. Few of us realize how powerfully urgency affects our choices. Urgency says, "I need it now!" "This cannot wait!" "I am in a jam, can you come right now?" Some of us get so use to the adrenaline rush of handling crises that we become dependent on it for a sense of energy. We get a temporary high from solving urgent crises. People expect us to be busy and overworked. It has become a status symbol in our society – if we are busy, we are important; if we are not busy, we are embarrassed to admit it.

Busyness is where we get our security and it is the primary excuse for not putting first things first in one's life. "I would love to spend quality time with you, but I have to work. There is a deadline. It is urgent!" Urgency addiction is a self-destructive behavior that temporarily fills the void created by unmet needs. We spend our lives dealing with squeaky wheels, rather than putting first things first.

Important things are those things that contribute to our overall objectives and gives richness and meaning to life. Important things do not tend to act upon us or press us, because they are not "urgent." They are simply things we must act upon. In my life it may be *urgent* to visit someone in the hospital, but it is *important* that I get to my daughter Danielle's school play. Urgency pulls you away from what is important if you are not careful. The urgent and the important are both a part of your life but you cannot constantly let the urgent direct the script of your life by default.

Access is the only influence that you have in your future. What you do with it determines where you will go and what you will accomplish. It is easy to be tempted to give your time to assorted activities. It is crucial to learn to keep your focus more narrowed so that you are able to give proper energy to your purpose while fulfilling your destiny.

Chapter 4

Your Success Is Determined By Those Who Have Access Into Your Life

Access will cause you to disconnect from anyone who does not celebrate your purpose. Personal relationships are more important than money or things. Your success is determined by those whom you let have access into your life. The book of Proverbs says, "Do not hang around an angry man or you will become angry." In other words, what you allow to have access in your life can distort your paradigm and cause you, in most cases, to adapt to their limited mindsets. Allow no one access who does not promote success. There are three types of people with whom you should sever access to your life immediately:

Poison People. Poison people are people who continually take from the relationship but never give. People either increase you or decrease you. If people are not adding to you, lifting you up, or encouraging you then they will inevitably take away from you. With poison people, it's all about them. They just suck the life right out of you. Every time they see you they ask, "How are you doing today? Have you heard what happened to me?" They do not even let you answer because they really do not care. The only reason they have a relationship with you is to drain your energy, breaking your focus and accomplishing their own agenda. Access will cause you to restrict limited thinkers from speaking into your life.

Judgmental People. Judgmental people are people who are always tearing others down because of their own shattered egos, pride, rebellion, and low self-esteem. Look at the word - people who judge are mental. Judgmental people will try to pass on a judgmental attitude. They are always tearing everything and everybody down. Matthew 7:1-6, says, "Do not judge or you too will be judged. For the same way you judge others, you will be judged. And with the measure you use, it will be measured to you. Why do you look at the speck of sawdust in your brother's eye and pay no attention to the plank in your eye? How can you say to your brother, 'let me get the speck out of your eye' when all the time there is a plank in your own eye? You hypocrite! First take the plank out of your own eye, and then you will see clearly to remove the speck from your brother's eye. Do not give dogs what is sacred and do not throw your pearls to pigs. If you do, they may trample them under their feet and then turn and tear you into pieces." Judgmental people will take your plans and ideas, what you are most passionate about, and tear them apart with their derogatory remarks.

Negative people. Negative people are the pessimists of life. In their attitude and speech nothing is ever good enough. They may have justifiable concerns but too often get involved in minor matters. They blame others and look for excuses. Even when blame can be justified it serves no productive good. They are usually negative because they have ceded control of their happiness to others.

If you find yourself surrounded by negative people, it is a good sign that you are negative. You might not even realize that you are negative. In most cases this type of attitude develops in your life from not having the knowledge to properly confront what the enemy throws at you.

How do you attract positive people into your life? You alter the way you speak, teach, and live by shifting to a positive paradigm. Matthew 12:33 says, "Make a tree good, and its fruit will be good. Make a tree bad and its fruit will be bad. For a tree will be recognized by its fruit. You brood of vipers! How can you who are evil say anything good? For out of the overflow of the heart the mouth speaks. The good man brings good things out of the good stored up in him and the evil man brings out evil things of the evil stored up in him. But I tell you that men will have to give an account on the Day of Judgment for every careless word they have spoken. For by your words you will be acquitted and by your words you will be condemned."

Negative emotions are anger, hate, and fear. They have absolutely nothing to do with the attributes of God and you need to replace them with faith, hope, and love.

You need to cut the accessibility of your time to those with these negative emotions.

By cutting access to these people you will limit what you hear and see so that what you desire is visible at all times. It is imperative that you pursue the plan, passion, desire and heartbeat of what God wants for you. You need to go after your destiny with everything that is within you. God has appointed people in your life to help you reach your destiny, but those people cannot get to you if you are continually letting the wrong people have access and take up your time. There are three people that you should definitely let have access into your life:

The Man of God. This could be a man or a woman of God, but for the sake of alliteration we are going to say man of God. God is a God of order and accountability, and He has placed someone in authority over you to be your spiritual covering. Matthew explains this principle in his gospel as he describes the story of the centurion, "Lord, I do not deserve to have you come under my roof. But just say the word, and my servant will be healed. For I myself am a man under authority, with soldiers under me. I tell this one, 'Go,' and he goes..." He understood the concept of submitting to authority, and therefore, Jesus declared him a man of great faith.

The only way you get the covering and protection that you need is by coming up under the man that God has placed in authority over you and submitting yourself to him. This is so that when he speaks, his words have power to bring about change in your life. II Chronicles 20:20 says, "… have faith in the Lord your God and you will be upheld; have faith in His prophets and you will be successful."

Mentors. There are two ways to learn - mistakes or mentors. I suggest a mentor. Proverbs 13:20 says, "He who walks with the wise grows wise, but a companion of fools suffers harm." Your friends are happy with the way you are but a mentor loves you too much to allow you to persist in your current way of life. A mentor is an experienced advisor or a supporter who watches over and fosters progress in another person.

There are two types of mentors- first, there are those who do not know you. Tommy Barnett is one of my mentors. I love Pastor Barnett and highly respect him. I believe he is an apostle to the nations, and that what he has done with the Dream Center, with his sons, and with his church is incredible. I have bought every book he has, and listen to his tapes continually. Tommy Barnett does not even know me. I have never shaken the man's hand, but he has invested in me. He is a master mentor in my life.

Secondly, there are mentors that you know. There are people like Dr. Paul Crites and Rev. Wayne Ralph in my life. These are men who have personally been involved in shaping my life and ministry. Their ministerial experiences have helped me to minister more effectively today. Their failures became my education and their accomplishments have given me an awareness that has propelled me to my own personal achievements.

If you want to be the best plumber in town, then find the best plumber in town and be his protégé. Carry his bag, carry his tools, and watch what he does. Ask him to pass on his skills to you then maybe one day, you will have somebody carrying your bags and your tools and you will be passing on to someone else how to be a master plumber. What you can access quickly determines its value in your life. It is your responsibility to control your access so that you can pursue your mentor. Your mentors must have unlimited access into your life.

Mature Believers. Mature believers are experienced men and women showing qualities gained by discipleship, development, and experience. One dictionary describes maturity as, "No longer subject to instability." I have been in the ministry for many years and I have seen people that have horrible marriages, financial predicaments, and emotional problems, and they are going to people who have even worse financial, emotional, and marital problems. The blind lead the blind and they both end up in the ditch. People go to all the wrong sources and end up with the wrong advice and then wonder why their lives are in such a mess. Search out a mature believer who has attained what you desire as your goal, someone with the authority, the ability, or the experience to change your life.

In your personal life, if you do not develop your own self-awareness and become responsible, if you do not seek God and find your God given destiny or purpose, you empower other people, and outside circumstances to shape much of your life by default. If you do not know your purpose you are wasting time, money, anointing, life, resources, and energy. It is in vain! It is like getting on a plane and having the pilot announce, "Folks we have good news and bad news. The good news is we are full of fuel the bad news is I do not have a clue where we are going, but we can hang out for a long time."

Who you give access to determines your success. Most people are too accessible. You do not make an appointment with a brain surgeon about a cavity. Not everyone with a problem has to have it fixed by you. Access controlled is your greatest treasure. Therefore you must learn to control who has access. There are three steps to limit and control access.

1. Evaluate. Not everyone should have access. Access will be misunderstood by others, so it is important that you evaluate the people that you have surrounding you. It is God's plan to staff your weaknesses. Look around you. What you need is hidden within the individuals that God has placed in your life. At the same time there are people who have been assigned to distract, delay, and discourage your focus by improper access. Your disadvantage will be the need for friendship so much that you will include anyone in your circle of friends no matter what they bring to the table. You must become skilled at discerning between the people who are sent by God (you have something they need, they have something you need) to assist you in fulfilling your destiny, and those who are assignments to discourage and distract you causing you to lose your focus on your future. Access will cause you to evaluate what is really needed around you for you to remain productive and focused.

2. Limit. Take responsibility for your destiny. Don't allow others to derail your progress by side tracking you with activities that rob you of your time. "Do you have a few minutes to talk about...?" We say, "yes" or "no" to things many times a day. A center of correct principles and a focus on your personal mission empowers you with wisdom to make those judgments effectively. Do not be misled. You are responsible for your choices. While some of these choices may seem small and insignificant at the time, these decisions join together to move you with increasing force toward your final destiny. Over time, your choices have become habits of the heart. More than any other factor, these habits of the heart affect your time and the quality of your life. Those who have access today may need to be limited tomorrow. There are people that need access to you but should not consume you. Protect your access by putting a time limit on every meeting. Ecclesiastes 8:5 says, "...the wise heart will know the proper time and procedure." Access will cause you to attack disorder and establish order. You must distinguish your position and priority in each and every relationship. Trying to accommodate everybody is a trap that will cause you to lose sight of your own priorities. Not everybody will listen to reason or even act in his or her own best interests, but you can. If you want to be happy and make your life meaningful you cannot allow access to unqualified people. Be polite and encouraging to unqualified people but learn to set limits to their access. You can be compassionate, and still be strong enough to offer a temporary safe haven without becoming a permanent home. As your relationship with those with limited access develops you may find that their limited thinking expands. Therefore there is greater return in the relationship allowing you to extend more access. In the same way those who have access today may need to be limited tomorrow. Remember you are responsible for your destiny. Access will discover what you really need around you to remain productive. Allow no one access who does not promote success.

3. Sever. E.M. Bounds said this, "The successful person has the habits of doing things failures don't like to do. The successful people don't necessarily like them either but their dislike is subordinate to their strength of purpose." To be successful you must be prepared to sever unhealthy relationships. Access will cause you to walk away from something you desire to protect something you love. Never stay in an atmosphere that eliminates your creativity. Friendships that do not fuel focus need to die. Even with patience and reason, all you may be able to do is to restate your position, set limits, and outline possible consequences. Finally, you may have no recourse except to back off. Your forceful persuasion may be elegant and logical to you but will probably do little to change someone who is unmotivated to change himself/herself. You do not have to sacrifice your life to the problems of people unwilling to change.

U.S. Navy Admiral Hyman Rickover said, "Great minds discuss ideas, average minds discuss events, small minds discuss people." There will be people who live in disorder, content with where they are in life, who will not understand your passion for your purpose. Your own family may not understand your passion. Access will cause you to have conflict in certain relationships in your life. It is not your mission to correct them, unless they are your assignment. If relationships become unconstructive then you must make a decision. Mark Twain said, "Keep away from people who try to belittle your ambitions. Small people always do that, but the really great make you feel that you, too, can become great." Follow the three steps above in every relationship. You will never acquire what you want to attain without being willing to pursue it with everything that is within you. Anybody who trivializes your passion is an enemy to your dream and destiny.

Chapter 5

Your Success is Determined by Those Whom You Let Have Access to Speak into Your Life

When E.F. Hutton speaks, the whole financial world listens. Why? Because he has proven that he has something to say about finances and economics. When Alan Greenspan, the Chairman of the Federal Reserve Board, speaks the whole economic world stops and listens. Their hearts skip a beat because what he says affects everybody. There is power in the spoken and heard word. Proverbs 18:21 says the tongue has the power of life and death. What is spoken into your life affects how you think and how you think affects how you act. What you hear is what you believe and what you believe is what you receive. This means you can either speak life or speak death. "Faith comes by hearing and hearing by the word of God."

You must also guard whom you let speak into your life. Access will cause you to limit what you hear and what you see so that what you desire is visible at all times. There are three people that you should not let speak into your life:

The Unfaithful. If someone is not faithful to work, to church, or to what God has called them to do, then surely God is not going to trust them with a word to change your life. People that are unfaithful are saved one day and backslid the next. Do not let them speak into your life because they will only speak life one day and death the next.

The Unfruitful. Paul said, "Entrust this teaching to reliable men and women who will teach it to others." Do not let people that are not producing fruit speak into your life. If they are not producing fruit, then they do not have the evidence that you need wisdom about; Go to someone who is showing the signs of wisdom and speak to them about it. Let them speak into your life.

The Unfocused. Anybody that desires to be successful is going to be criticized and slandered by people who are unfocused. Failures hate successes. When you focus your attention and time on achieving success you cannot allow those who are not focused to steal your time and speak limiting thoughts into your life. The unfocused person just wants to talk. They have no plan. Focus is magnetic. If the unfocused consumes your access, you too will become unfocused.

You must guard both the words you say and those that you allow others to speak over you. Proverbs 13:3 says, "He who guards his lips guards his life, but he who speaks rashly, his life will come to ruin." Words are powerful. Every word that is spoken plants a seed. You can either plant seeds that create a positive mind-set or you can plant seeds that create a negative one.

The people that are allowed access to you either speak positive words or negative words that can affect your success. You must understand that not only are you accountable for every word you have said, but you also have to deal with what people have said to and about you. That is why it is so important to guard who you allow access into your life. When people speak doubt over your life it is a planted seed. Most of the people in prison where told by their parents on countless occasions, "If you keep doing what you're doing, you'll end up in jail one day." And you know what they do? They live up to the expectations that were spoken over them.

You need to guard your mouth, so that your life can be guarded. Change the way you speak. Speak faith to your children. Speak faith to your spouse. Speak faith to your future. When you wake up in the morning apply the blood of Jesus Christ to your mind, body, soul, and spirit so that you can guard what you say and protect yourself from the negative words of others directed at you. It is important to allow access only to those who contribute to a positive mind-set thereby promoting success, and providing focus to help draw you toward your destiny.

Final Thoughts

The thing that encumbers our success the most is fear. FEAR is defined as - False Evidence Appearing Real. The University of Michigan conducted a study which showed the following: 60% of our fears are totally unwarranted; they never come to pass. 20% of our fears are focused on our past, which is completely out of our control. 10% of our fears are based on things so petty that they make no difference in our lives. Of the remaining 10%, only 4-5% could be considered justifiable. What this tells us is that 95% of our fears are unproductive. You think it is going to hurt you but it is not. God is in control and God is going to help you. You must replace your fear with faith. Faith is action. I want you to act in faith and to begin to produce tangible results for your success.

Staying focused on controlling access leads to your success. That is the truth! But the application of this revelation is the hard part. If being successful were easy, everybody would be successful. I want to give you some keys so that the principles in this book are more than just principles.

Access must be given to your secret place to meet with God. To hear the voice of God you must move away from the voices of others. Allowing God access will open the doors of impartation into your life. The only way you can develop intimacy with God is to pull away from others. When you pull away from others you allow God to impart into your life. Impartation is essential for change. God wants to increase His access in your life.

Access must be given to discover your destiny. If you don't seek God and find your God given destiny or purpose, you empower other people and circumstances outside to shape much of your life by default. Until you have a compelling destiny for your life, you just exist. What motivates you to get out of bed everyday? What keeps you going? Discovering your destiny. Destiny will draw out of you God given abilities and make you more than you could be on your own. It is something that pulls you towards a goal. It does not drive you, it draws you. You have to discover your destiny. Access will cause you to stop thinking about and looking at where you are and cause you to speak and plan where you want to be. You must build your daily agenda around your destiny.

Access must be given everyday to your principle priorities. When you give your time for something, you are giving your life. That is what life is made up of -- your time. We tend to think that the most important thing we can give people is our money. Money can be replaced. But when you give people your time, that is irreplaceable. Great people are just ordinary people who have made a distinctive dedication to a distinguished destiny.

Access must be given to your mentors. Proverbs 15:22 says, "Plans fail for lack of counsel, but with many advisers they succeed." Your mentors impart wisdom through relationship. A mentor will see what you do not see, and love you enough to correct it. You must pursue the mentor for what he has learned not earned. You cannot have reputation without preparation. Respect access to your mentor's time by using the time you have together wisely.

Access must be given to your assignments. Tom Landry said, "I make men do what they don't want to do so that they can become what they want to be." Somewhere somebody is assigned to you. A mentor is someone you learn from. A protégé is someone assigned to learn from you. Your assignment is a relationship divinely appointed by God; it is always to a person or to a people. Remember you are not called to everybody; you are called to somebody. It is your protégé's responsibility to pursue you and it is your responsibility to control access in a way that allows maximum benefit and preparation of the protégé. Spend time in your secret place asking the Holy Spirit for wisdom in developing your assignment.

You must decide what to do with the information you

have just been given. No one can force you to change. To be successful you must focus on applying the revelation not just expanding your information. "Knowledge of what's possible is the beginning of happiness", wrote American Philosopher and Poet George Santayana. However, success is the achievement of something that you have planned for or have attempted. It takes more than just knowledge; you must have a plan, a purpose. Let this be your moment. Now is your time. There is no other. Find a purpose for your life that you can follow with passion. Yes, you want to be financially independent. Yes, you want good health. Yes, you want strong bonds to family and friends. Yes, you can become tough, kind, rich, and have it all. Your actions will make that decision. George Bernard Shaw pointed out, "Progress is impossible without change, and those who cannot change their minds cannot change anything." Access is the key to your purpose. Access is the key to progress. **Therefore, access is the key to success!**

Discovering Your Destiny

Four questions you must ask to reveal your destiny.

1. What do I love? _____

_____

_____

_____

_____

2. What do I hate or angers me? _____

_____

_____

_____

_____

3. What makes me cry or grieves me?_____

_____

_____

_____

_____

4. What irritates me? _____

_____

_____

_____

_____

- **what you love reveals the gifts you contain.**
- **what you hate reveals what you are called to correct.**
- **what makes you cry reveals what you are called to heal.**
- **what irritates you reveals the problem you've been assigned.**

Using less than 21 words, state your destiny: _____

_____

_____

Allowing Access

The man of God in my life is

_____

_____

_____

_____

My mentors are

_____

_____

_____

_____

My assignment is

_____

_____

_____

_____

People that need to have limited access to me

_____

_____

_____

_____

I will pursue my mentor by

_____

_____

_____

_____

Fulfilling Your Destiny

Goals to fulfill my destiny (my daily priorities should lead me to my goal)

_____

_____

_____

_____

People that are assigned to help me

_____

_____

_____

_____

I will develop my assignment by

_____

_____

_____

_____

I will give God more access by

_____

_____

_____

_____

My principal priorities are

_____

_____

_____

_____

Things I need to
remove/delegate/improve/set aside

40 Points of Access

1. Access is giving the right to encounter or exchange with someone, and you hold the keys to that access.

2. Access is the control of time and time is your life.

3. Access controlled is your greatest treasure.

4. Access is not time management, it is self management.

5. Access, like purpose and passion, must be protected.

6. Access focuses on your application of the revelation, not just the expansion of the information.

7. Access must be given to discover your destiny.

8. Access will cause you to focus on the difference between the important and the urgent.

9. Access will cause you to allow no one exchange who does not promote success.

10. Access will allow you to detect those assigned to distract, delay, and discourage your focus.

11. Access given to the wrong or unwanted person will hinder your productivity.

12. Access will keep you focused on your assignment.

13. Access given to someone who is not your assignment is dangerous.

14. Access is the only influence that you have over your future.

15. Access must be given to your assignment. If you give the wrong person access then the right person cannot get to you.

16. Access requires intense planning.

17. Access will cause organization of schedules and appointments.

18. Access will cause you to delegate tasks to others.

19. Access will cause you to disconnect from anyone who does not celebrate your purpose.

20. Access granted today may need to be limited tomorrow.

21. Access will help you recognize important gifts in your life.

22. Access will cause you to celebrate those you love.

23. Access will open doors of impartation in your life.

24. Access must be protected and given to your secret place to meet with God.

25. Access plans for the unexpected.

26. Access will cause conflict in relationships in your life.

27. Access will be misunderstood by others.

28. Access must be given to your mentors.

29. Access must be given everyday to your principle priorities.

30. Access will not allow you to draw yesterday into your future.

31. Access will cause you to attack disorder and establish order.

32. Access will create an atmosphere of creativity.

33. Access will cause you to evaluate what is really needed around you for you to remain productive and focused.

34. Access will cause you to limit what you hear and what you see so that what you desire is visible at all times.

35. Access will cause you to walk away from some thing you desire to protect something you love.

36. Access will cause you to stop thinking about and looking at where you are and cause you to speak and plan where you want to be.

37. Access will cause you to restrict limited thinkers from speaking into your life.

38. Access will eliminate any appointment or request that does not qualify for your focus.

39. Access will motivate passion and enthusiasm for your assignment.

40. Access forces the exit of wrong people and things opening the door to right people and things.

Better Hope Ministries

David K. Crawford, Author, Counselor, Pastor of River Community Church and Founder and President of Destiny Christian College has dedicated his life to educating and inspiring people, empowering them to rise above their circumstances and equipping them to effect their destiny.

Since his powerful conversion as a teenager, Pastor Crawford's ministry has blessed thousands. His life transforming message of a better hope has taken him from the backwoods to boardrooms, from the pulpits of America to the platforms of TV studios, colleges and conferences around the World.

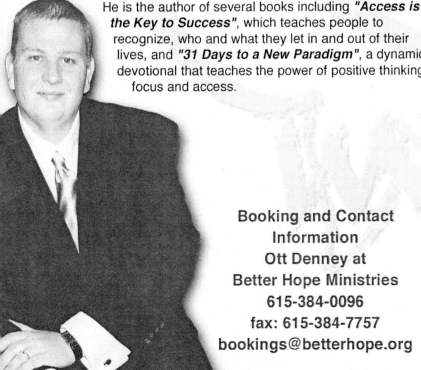

He is the author of several books including *"Access is the Key to Success"*, which teaches people to recognize, who and what they let in and out of their lives, and *"31 Days to a New Paradigm"*, a dynamic devotional that teaches the power of positive thinking, focus and access.

**Booking and Contact
Information
Ott Denney at
Better Hope Ministries
615-384-0096
fax: 615-384-7757
bookings@betterhope.org**

No matter what your age is, no matter where you come from, no matter who you are, there is a place for you at River Community Church. You'll meet a great mix of friendly people, hear relevant messages, enjoy compelling programs and much more. Come as you are, be who you are-we've got a seat saved for you. Whatever your need, we have the answer. Whatever your interests, you can find your joy here.

Senior Pastor David K. Crawford

Service Times

Sunday Morning Service	9:30 am
River Kids Service	9:30 am
Sunday Night Service	6:00 pm
Upstream Youth Wednesday	7:00 pm
540 Fridays Youth	7:00 pm

River
COMMUNITY
CHURCH

Church Location: 1033 Bradley Drive, Springfield TN
Phone: 615-384-0096 Fax: 615-384-7757
Office Hours Monday-Thursday 9:00 a.m. to 5:00 p.m.

Our Purpose:

The 4:11 Network is a kingdom relationship based organization of five-fold ministries and market-place ministers providing apostolic activation through credentials, covering, connection and on going mentorship.

4:11 Network Members Benefits

- Credentials - Licenses and Ordination
- Accredited Distance Learning
- Insurance Programs
- Monthly Mentorship
- Annual Convention
- Regional Leadership Training
- Placement & Internship Programs
- Church Planting Programs
- International Mission Trips
- Publishing House Discounts
- Assistance in Securing 501C3 Exempt Status

Dr. Paul Crites
Apostle and Executive Bishop of The 4:11 Network

P.O. Box 952 · Springfield, TN 37172 · 615.384.4391
615.384.7757 fax · email: 411network@mail.com

identity

purpose

impact

At Prosperity Designs, our vision is to generate materials to impact your desired target. With advertisement designs, mass marketing mail out designs, special event packages and church identity packages, each one geared especially for your special needs.

A professionally designed identity package is the key to your impact, because you only get one chance to make a good first impression.

Prosperity

designs

prosperitydesign@mail.com

DESTINY CHRISTIAN COLLEGE

Destiny Christian College offers quality training for the serious student who desires to gain a better understanding of God's Word, and share the gospel message in this generation. The Spirit of God is releasing new and creative ways to increase the kingdom of God. Destiny Christian College is a God given tool to help accomplish this purpose. Come and be equipped and activated into ministry to go forth into the harvest that awaits us. We are committed to the student's growth and increase through three key areas: **Mentorship, Modeling and Impartation.**

ASSOCIATE DEGREE
Christian Leadership

CERTIFICATE
Biblical Studies

For More Information:
Destiny Christian College
P.O. Box 952
Springfield, TN 37172
615.384.4391 fax: 615.384.7757
destinycollege@betterhope.org

Your Letter is Very Important to Me

You are very special to me, and I believe that you are special to God. I want to assist you in any way possible. Write me when you need an intercessor to pray for you. When you write, my staff and I will pray over your letter. I will write back.

Pastor Crawford, please enter into the prayer of agreement with me for the following needs:
(please print)

_____

_____

_____

_____

_____

_____

_____

_____

_____

_____

_____

_____

_____

_____

_____

_____

_____

mail to:
Better Hope Ministries
P.O. Box 952 Springfield, TN 37172
615.384.0096 fax: 615.384.7757

Decision

Will you accept Jesus as your personal savior today?

Knowing your sins are forgiven and you are ready for heaven is as simple as following these steps:

Admit you have sinned.
"For all have sinned and fall short of the glory of God" (Romans 3:23)

Believe in Jesus.
"For God so loved the world that He gave His one and only Son, that whoever believes in Him shall not perish but have eternal life" (John 3:16)

Confess and leave your sin behind.
"If we confess our sins, he is faithful and just and will forgive us our sins and purify us from all unrighteousness" (1John 1:9)

☐ *Yes, Pastor Crawford, I made a decision to accept Christ as my personal Savior today!*

Name_____

Address _____

City_____ State_____

Zip_____

mail to:
Better Hope Ministries
P.O. Box 952 Springfield, TN 37172